Good-Bye My Friend

Pet Cemeteries, Memorials, and Other Ways to Remember

A Collection of Thoughts, Feelings, and Resources

IRVINE, CALIFORNIA

by Michele Lanci-Altomare

Ruth Strother, project manager
Nick Clemente, special consultant
Amy Fox, copy editor

Endpapers photograph: Dog Graves at Leeds Castle, Maidstone, Kent, England

Library of Congress Cataloging-in-Publication Data

Lanci-Altomare, Michele, 1962-
Good-bye my friend : pet cemeteries, memorials, and other ways to remember : a collection of thoughts, feelings, and resources / Michele Lanci-Altomare.
p. cm.
Includes bibliographical references.
ISBN 1-889540-57-9 (hardcover : alk. paper)
1. Pet cemeteries--United States. 2. Pet cemeteries--England. I. Title.
SF414.5 .L36 2000
636.088'7--dc21
00-009258

For more information on creative use techniques (image transfer, emulsion transfer or SX-70 manipulation), please contact Polaroid's Customer Care Center at 1-800-343-5000 or visit Polaroid's Web site at: www.polaroid.com/prophoto.

BowTie ™ Press
A Division of Fancy Publications
3 Burroughs
Irvine, California 92618

Manufactured in the United States of America
10 9 8 7 6 5 4 3 2 1

From now til the end of time,

I will be grateful to Nick Altomare my husband, soulmate, and best friend. Thank you for always believing in me and my creative path, and for never raising an eyebrow at my elaborate ideas or travel plans. If it wasn't for your everlasting love and support, I would not have been able to complete this exciting journey. Thanks for being right beside me, no matter how intense the ride became!

Special thanks go to Mel and Tom Lanci, my parents, for supporting my artistic career from the beginning, and for teaching me at a very young age what it means to love and care for an animal friend. Thanks for showing me the life and beauty in cemeteries as a child. To Angela Lanci-Macris my sister and Jim Macris my brother-in-law for always being available to offer advice, encouragement, creative opinions, map orientation, and a warm, cozy second home for Vinnie when Nick and I were off to faraway lands. Thanks Lil! To Charlie Motta, my grandfather, for always being there no matter what, and for providing me with the most accurate representation of the human-animal bond that I have ever seen. To Helen Altomare, my mother-in-law, for being willing to travel no matter how wet it was! To Mark and Marisa Caropreso, my cousins, for all the adventures—including those that were animal related. To Aunt Babe and Uncle Tony for all the frogs. To Denise McCoy for my first creative opportunity. To everyone associated with BowTie Press, especially Ruth Strother who believed in my work enough to encourage the publishing of this book and gave me endless hours and countless days of guidance, and Nick Clemente for his passion, enthusiasm, and loyalty. Thank you Norman Ridker, Amy Fox, Gary Mah, Mike Uyesugi, Tonya Adams, Debbie Phillips-Donaldson, Jon Rosenberg, David Bolhuis, and Wendy Pratt for your dedication to this project. Pat Blosser, where do I begin? Thank you from the bottom of my heart for your patience and generosity in keeping the information free flowing. To Brenda Drown for the list and for helping me verify all the information. A special thanks goes to Peter Drown for all the help at the beginning stages of this project. Rest in peace, Peter. I'm sorry you passed away before seeing the final result of this book. To Rosie Lukenda, those two phone numbers helped me immensely. To Les Green for spreading the word and for the web referrals from around the world! To all the IAPC members and pet cemeterians who so generously offered information and welcomed me, my cameras, and my travel partners to their locations with open arms. To Del and Sue Howison of Dark Delicacies for promoting and showcasing my photography in the Los Angeles area for the past several years. To Claude Hulce and Carol Finkle of the Creative Arts Center Gallery in Burbank, and to Phil Lohman and Scott Canty of the Palos Verdes Art Center for providing me with beautiful gallery spaces to hold my solo photographic exhibitions. To John Richardson and Ron Smith for the constant expert photographic advice. To Pat Dejura and the Polaroid Corporation for your generous gift of film. I needed it!

And to all my friends: Janis Unterweiser, Lori Palmer, Rebecca Bright, Mary Ann and Phil Beals, Mick Wainman, Maureen and Chris Warner, Katherine Caldwell, Diane and Jim Fallon, Ellen Lawlor and Jim Brown, Jordan Kratz, Al Palmer, Rochelle and Scott Grant, Bert and June Gader, Lucy J. Kim, Pat McFarlin, Paul Butler, Tom and Ana Londergan, Karen Stewart, Sid Cook, Anthony Hasler, JoAnn and Victor Boyce, Rick Penn-Kraus, Heather Parlato, Paula Lang, Cyndi Finkle, Amy Inouye, Linda Heichman, and Jo Jo Gibert, whether you've been by my side since the early days, helped support my photographic career in recent times, worked on this project with me, took care of my animals, modeled for me, traveled with me, held the umbrella, looked at the map (or at least attempted to), took notes, carried the camera bag, hauled the tripod, provided a place for me to sleep, lent a listening ear, or patiently put up with my presence (or lack thereof) during this adventure, thank you. If there's anyone I've left out, I'm sorry, it wasn't intentional—you all hold a special place in my heart.

Grandma Betty Motta and Grandpa Camillo Lanci, thank you for being there—still.
Your lives and deaths affected my existence more than you will ever know.

Dedicated to LeRoy Altomare

1986 – 1997

I miss you, good friend.

Thanks for sharing your life with me.

Until next time,

R. I. P.

From as far back as I can remember, animals have been a part of my life. As a child, I had all kinds of pets. Many of them were not my very own and didn't actually live in my house, but we shared unique experiences. Some were just visitors, such as the neighborhood dogs who were allowed to roam freely and would run alongside me as I peddled my bike. Some lived indoors, such as the black-and-white cats who lived in the corner house. They'd rub their heads and press their bodies against the screen from the inside as I pressed my hand against it from the outside. Others were weekend pets, such as the semiferal cats who lived adjacent to my Grandpa Lanci's apartment complex or the reptiles and birds who were part of the permanent collection at Woolworth's. A lot of my "outdoor" pets were the kind who would cause most people to feel creepy or shriek in fear of getting bitten. All creatures, whether they were spiders, caterpillars, frogs, and even jellyfish, were precious beings to me.

My fondest memories are of our family "Kat," Missy. I emphasize the word *cat* with a capital *K* because Missy wasn't just a cat. For nineteen years, Missy truly reigned as King of the jungle—even if the jungle was just upstate New York. She bestowed upon us live gifts of eyeless moles and tailless chipmunks, baby robins and blue jays, and once she presented us with an entire litter of baby rabbits, one by one by one. Missy truly was a giver. She usually didn't take animals' lives—she merely borrowed them. It was almost like she knew we would welcome them into our home too.

Most often, Mom was the one to be rewarded with Missy's gifts. My sister, Angela, and I enjoyed coming to the rescue and taking care of these injured animals. It was always exciting for us to come home and see a new cardboard box on the deck—what kind of surprise would be inside? Dad just went along with it all, hoping these little critters would eventually be strong enough to be set free and escape beyond Missy's kingdom. Angela used rocks as markers to create a cemetery at the edge of the woods for all of Missy's gifts who didn't survive. No matter how you look at it, this is nature—life and death—and I'm glad to have had these experiences at a young age.

Throughout my life, I spent quite a bit of time with my family going to the cemetery, which, except for the actual funerals of Grandpa Lanci and Grandma Motta, was not usually a sad or dramatic event. It was pretty enjoyable. We'd take a ride to the cemetery on special holidays or on nice Sunday afternoons after getting ice cream cones. We'd pick up the old flowers, replace them with fresh ones, and then look around to see which new neighbors had arrived and how they were related to all the other

Missy Lanci
1969-1987

people we knew on that hill. Although these visits forced us to realize how much we missed our loved ones' physical presence, our trips to the cemetery were always something we looked forward to.

Developing an early appreciation for the necropoli, or the cities of the dead, definitely contributed to my focus on these locations when I began my photographic studies in college. My creative adventure wasn't so different from my peers', for I was on the "still life" path too! Since the early 1980s, I've traveled all over the U.S., also taking side trips to England, Scotland, Wales, Italy, and Paris to photograph cemeteries. I tend to end up in locations that are somewhat overgrown and unkempt—places that attract a lot of wild animals such as deer, large birds, raccoons, and also cats.

Cats like these places. It seems to be a safe haven for them, especially in the larger locations where there are big monuments for them to seek shelter in. They can be protected from bad weather, have a lot of mysterious hiding places, can perch atop a large cross, or look regal on the head of a large-winged angel. And, they can follow me around! I have so many shots of cats in my cemetery images—especially the ones from Rome.

During these excursions through human cemeteries, I occasionally stumbled upon pet cemeteries. As time went on, it happened more and more frequently. Then I began looking for them everywhere I went. My focus had changed. I had combined my love for both subjects—animals and cemeteries. Some of the pet cemeteries were absolutely gorgeous. Stunning large pieces of land, blankets of velvety green grass, surrounded by ornate flowering plants and gardens, wrought iron gates, granite benches, decorative fountains, bird baths, ponds—nature everywhere. The more I searched, the more I found. The more I found, the more I read. The more I read the inscriptions on the grave markers, the more I cried, and I cried a lot. It was painful

Protestant Cemetery
Rome, Italy

to read these statements of love and loss. Sure, I read the epitaphs in many of the human cemeteries I ventured through, but they weren't like these. Even the old New England skull-and-crossbones tombstones with their graphic poetics didn't have the painful energy that these animal monuments had.

It didn't take me long to realize that animal companionship has a deep impact not only on me, but on just about all human life that it touches. Now that my vision had been directed toward pet cemeteries, I was starting to see something different. Something I never really noticed in human cemeteries. Something powerful. It was clear that the lives of these little animals often provide more profound relationships to humans than we humans provide for each other.

I thought about Missy again, and how she was always there for me. She knew when I was sad or lonely, and she couldn't stand to see me cry. When I moved away from my parent's house, Missy never held it against me for leaving her—when I returned to visit, she always treated me as though I had never left. I smiled when I thought about Jake my spiny tailed lizard, and how he'd always be so happy to see me when I walked into the room. Since he loved being on his leash outdoors, I'd try to take him out every day, but if I was unable to, he didn't become aggressive toward me. He was always affectionate and grateful for the time we spent together. I remembered my tarantulas, who provided me with so much pleasure, just being able to watch their mysterious intrigue and beauty. I reflected on my hamsters and guinea pigs—it was so much fun for the cats and me to watch them in all their quirkiness when they played so freely.

My memories shifted, and I thought about my first few pets and how we buried them in the yard. I smiled to myself when I thought about Angela and our cousin Mark when they were four years old accidentally killing Mark's goldfish (they took him out of the bowl to "clean" him with napkins), and the flushing ceremony we had to have. I started to feel sad when I thought about the day that Vito, my iguana, died. It was so hard for me to accept the fact that he wasn't just "playing dead." How could he be dead? He was fine a couple of minutes ago. He was well fed, took supplements, had plenty of space, got a lot of exercise. I kept tapping his strong body, trying to get him to wake up, calling his name louder and louder, but he didn't respond. That memory triggered thoughts of Beverly, my little ribbon snake who died in my hands. It was traumatic for me. She had some little tumors, but I hadn't expected her to die. It was hard for me to let go of her thin little eight-inch body. Then it hit me like a ton of bricks. How could I ever forget LeRoy, the voice that no longer speaks?

LeRoy
At Eight Months Old

He was black like the sky,
on a new moon night
and shined like the ocean
under a full moon's light

He had accents of white
like winter days bright
and eyes colored yellow
like summer sunlight.

My husband, Nick, and I met LeRoy in the fall of 1986, at a shelter in Salem, Massachusetts. Little did we know then that this tuxedoed cat would provide us with so many exciting and interesting events. But he knew. In fact, he knew the minute he saw us that we would be his. Life with LeRoy was never silent or dull. He appointed himself in charge of many different tasks, sometimes holding titles of high position and authority. All of them involved some sort of communication, usually verbal.

He spoke for our other animal companions in the morning and evening when it was time to eat. His cries were enormous when the potato was ablaze in the microwave oven. *I saved my home!* With panic in his voice he'd summon us to the bathtub so we could view the impending flood. *Shut that water off, now!* He'd sit by the living room window and cackle really low to the cats in the hood who'd gather outside and listen intently to what he said. When it was time to turn in, he'd purr like a Harley and call us to lie down in the big, comfy bed—his reward as the protector of his home. In a brief twelve years and at least nine lives later, LeRoy was silenced. By cancer. He verbalized nothing. His eyes spoke for him. The silence was final.

It's black like the sky,
on a new moon night
and shines like the ocean
under a full moon's light.

This little urn sits on my desk,
with him inside,
at eternal rest.

LeRoy's death was devastating. He was a true friend who shared my life. I had lost friends before, but this was different.

Throughout our lives, we make many friends. But how many friends are in our lives unconditionally? How many friends remain constant through thick and thin, no matter what? How many friends stick around when life gets difficult? How many friends can forgive and forget, and won't judge us because of our mistakes and faults? I bet everyone can answer these questions with a quick, *Not many!* I can, too.

Today, my feline companions Norman, Billy, and Venus allow Vinnie our boxer, Nick, and me to share their home. They are true, constant friends, and I cannot imagine life without them. LeRoy is with us in spirit in his beautiful porcelain urn. Maybe I made the decision to keep him near me because I couldn't imagine life without him either. I can still feel his presence. Even though my travels have allowed me to experience many beautiful and unique resting places, it's still hard for me to preplan for my animal companions' departures. When thoughts of the inevitable enter my mind, all I can do is remind myself of the many options of which I'm now aware. Within these pages you will see how I've been inspired by the warm, loving treatment others have given their pets. I hope this book inspires you too.

We welcome animals into our homes as new members of the family. We find veterinarians to care for their health. We teach our pets manners and even take some of them to school for obedience training. They are our children, our brothers and sisters, our best friends. We care for all aspects of our pets' brief stay on this earth. But even as they reach their senior years, becoming gray in the face, weak in the legs from arthritis, or stricken with a terminal illness, we find it difficult to plan for the day when they will no longer be with us. Although the life span of most of the animals we choose to share our lives with is short compared to ours, the memories are everlasting. Sharing one's life with a pet is a fulfilling and unique experience in love and companionship.

By looking back on the years of love and care we have given to our pets and the lifetime of companionship and devotion they have returned to us, we cherish their memories long after their lives end. There is no such thing as *just* an animal or *only* an iguana or *merely* a dog. These are friendships based on unconditional love. We truly merge our lives with these beings. Letting go of that partnership can be a devastating, difficult, and painful process. If you have ever lost a pet, you know what a big emptiness death can bring.

When a pet dies, we experience many difficult emotions. We may experience strong feelings of sadness, tiredness, loss of appetite, insomnia, forgetfulness, disinterest in previously enjoyed activities, withdrawal from others, and increased anxiety. The sense of loss, loneliness, guilt, or depression may be overwhelming, but the grieving process is a painful yet necessary part of living and loving. We need time for this pain to heal. The amount of time we each need varies because we all experience grief in our own ways. The bond that was created with a beloved companion has been broken. This loss is devastating.

Most people also feel the physical loss of their pets in the home. It may take some time to put a pet's things away, and there may be instances when we briefly forget a pet is no longer with us. It is common to feel guilty about a loss and to blame someone, even ourselves, for what has happened, especially if we had to struggle with the difficult decision of euthanasia. We might even become angry with our veterinarians, friends, and loved ones, thinking that no one truly understands.

Many times we repress our feelings of grief for a pet because we're afraid it is not "normal" to grieve so deeply over an animal. Some people discount the pain of grief because the loved one was not human. But psychologists say that the human response to loss is the same whether the loss is of a person or a pet. When your pet dies, it's important to surround yourself with people who understand your loss. Don't be ashamed or try to hide your grief. Grief denied is grief retained; the longer it is denied the longer you will grieve. Tears are an important part of accepting and working through the grief. Allow yourself to feel. Talk about your pain and feelings with family members and friends. It is just as normal and healthy to grieve over the loss of a pet as it is to grieve over the loss of a human.

The medical field is becoming far more aware of the deep bond between people and their pets. Support groups and grief recovery therapists are evolving rapidly. The purpose of a support group is to assist people in validating the loss of their pets, help them learn about their grief, and offer sound advice on how to handle the emotions surrounding the loss they have suffered. Ask your veterinarian about support groups in your area.

Grieving over the death of pets is not new. Since the beginning of time, animals have been a part of everyday human life, and honoring a pet in death was commonplace. For example, cats were respected to the point of adoration in some cultures. The cat achieved goddess status at about 1500 B.C. (and held on to that status until about 350 A.D.) as she became the figurehead for the Egyptian cat cult. Bastet, the cat icon of the goddess of feminine qualities, was worshipped and celebrated. In tribute to Bastet, the Egyptians bejeweled their domestic cats from head to toe and allowed them to dine from their people's dishes.

It's not surprising, then, that these early humans went to great lengths when a pet passed away. Not only did the Egyptians shave their eyebrows (they shaved their whole bodies when a dog passed) and go into deep mourning, but the cats were embalmed and anointed in sacred houses, mummified, and laid to rest in elaborate tombs. Most of the deceased animals were vaulted with food, so they wouldn't go hungry in the afterlife, in cat or dog cemeteries outside of the city. Bereaved family members would return to the grave with fish or milk for years to come. A few carved wooden cases containing cat mummies bound in colorful bandages with intricately marked facemasks still survive today. Elsewhere in the ancient world, Chinese emperors kept a dog cemetery at Peking with tombstones of marble, gold, and silver. Other countries have continued to carry on similar traditions.

Currently, there are pet cemeteries throughout the entire world: England, Scotland, France, and Russia, to name a few. In fact, in the U.S. alone there are more than four hundred active pet cemeteries that are in good operating condition. According to the International Association of Pet Cemeteries (IAPC), the oldest known pet cemetery was uncovered in Green County, Illinois, by archaeologist Dr. Stewart Schrever, who believes the pets were interred there around 6500 B.C. The oldest operating pet cemetery in the U.S. is the Hartsdale Pet Cemetery in New York, which was established in 1896. The largest pet cemetery in the U.S. is Bide-A-Wee Home Association, also located in New York. Some pet cemeteries today operate in conjunction with other pet-related businesses: boarding kennels, grooming salons, training centers, and veterinary hospitals. Some human cemeteries have set aside a portion of their grounds for pet burials.

Despite differences in religion, race, finances, and social status, those who choose to memorialize their pets have one thing in common—they are thoughtful people of integrity who have lost a good friend. When you are ready, you may choose a pet cemetery as the final resting place for your animal companion. Or, because you had a unique relationship with this friend, you may choose another unique way of memorializing your pet. By creating a special location to acknowledge, depict, and honor your pet's life, you have exhibited everlasting commemoration of your lost friend. Just remember that whatever you decide to do with your loved one is your choice. No one else can make that decision for you.

Egyptian cat mummy from Abydos. Roman Period, after 30 B.C.
Courtesy of the British Museum

In 1881, Hyde Park Pet Cemetery in London started as a garden kept by Victoria Lodge gatekeeper Mr. Winbridge, an employee of the Duke of Cambridge. A Maltese terrier named Cherry was the first burial. Graceful, elegant, and dandified, he was an accomplished dog of the world and delighted in giving drawing room entertainments.

"Some people may object that the custom of burying dogs and of establishing a regular dogs' cemetery is one that may develop into a danger to public health. But this idea is fallacious. Dogs are not buried in lead coffins, but in sacks or plain boxes. The danger of human cemeteries arises from the preservation of the bodies in lead coffins. In the earth-to-earth system, for instance, there is no danger, and dogs are buried on what is practically the earth-to-earth system."

—"A Cemetery for Dogs" written in 1893 by E.A. Brayley Hodgetts for The Strand *magazine.*

According to the Royal Parks Agency, the cemetery was officially closed in 1903 because it was full. Since then, there have been a few unofficial burials, one of which took place in 1954.

Leeds Castle
Dog Grave
Maidstone, Kent • England

Hyde Park
Pet Cemetery
London • England

Broward Pet Cemetery and Crematory
Plantation, Florida

Initially, the prayer at graveside would choke me up—still does occasionally. It gratifies me to listen and offer sympathy to clients as they talk about their deceased companions—I think it helps them get through this very trying time. There once was a family who bought a bubble maker to the cemetery, and after the service, when my staff and I had walked away, they blew bubbles into the air above the grave—obviously a game they played with their dog when he was alive.

—Ernest E. Seiler, Jr., D.V.M., Broward Pet Cemetery and Crematory

Craig Road Pet Cemetery,
Funeral Home, and Crematoriums
Las Vegas, Nevada

Bubbling Well
Pet Memorial Park
Napa, California

Pet Haven Cemetery and Crematory
Ooltewah, Tennessee

The most difficult part of my job is preparing the animals for burial. I try to help people feel okay about their grief. I cry with them. Some people come weekly to visit their deceased pet, others not so often. There is one gentleman who comes every week to share a beer with his deceased dog.

When one of my dogs passed away, the loss was worse than when I lost my parents. Friends helped me through my grief. My pets have been cremated, so I've taken them with me when I've moved. I still feel a sense of their presence—very much so. I talk to them daily in my living room.

—Vivian E. Miller, Noah's Ark Boarding Kennel and Pet Cemetery

Pet Heaven
Memorial Park
Miami, Florida

Paw Print Gardens
Pet Cemetery and Crematory
West Chicago, Illinois

Charlie and Bingo
Early 1950s

Mella, Bingo, and Babe
Early 1950s

At eighty-six years old, I have two animal friends I will never forget. Bingo was a good dog. In earlier years, he instinctively knew when I was due home. He would insist on going outside to wait for me on our front steps, so he could watch down the street for the bus to drop me off. When my daughters, Babe and Mella, were around six to eight years old, Bingo would accompany them to school. One of the classrooms was visible from a ground-level window. He would sit at that window and watch. Eventually, the teacher felt that Bingo was distracting the class because all the kids wanted to be near the window, so she would send my older girl home to return the dog. My daughter would cry all the way home because she didn't want to leave school. Bingo would lick the tears from her face because he couldn't stand to see her cry. We'd leave him in the house for at least an hour after she went back to school, but no matter what, he'd always end up back at that school again, later in the day. He'd put his nose to the ground, and follow her scent right back there.

Many years later, we were prepared for Bingo's death because our veterinarian was treating him for kidney failure. It was sorrowful. He was a faithful friend, and in his final years would lay under the cash register stand in my barbershop while I cut hair. After he died, his presence still remained. That was forty-three years ago. Time heals your wounds—but slowly.

Buffy, my red tabby cat, would lay on my chest every time I laid down to watch television, and when she wanted my attention, she would nudge me under my chin with her head until I started talking to her—then she was content. That cat was really something. One time she climbed the oak tree in the back, on the edge of the gully. She wouldn't come down, so we had to get a 40-foot extension ladder, and I had to climb a good 4 feet after that! I was able to bring her down, but I could have really fallen!

Another time, we saw her dragging her back legs as she tried to cross the street. Come to find out, she had a broken pelvis, a broken leg, and a broken tail. She had to have her tail removed, but the rest healed well. A car or a minibike must have hit her. We kept her secluded underneath the playpen for a good six weeks. She was feisty—you couldn't keep her inside, even after that. She'd come home all cut up—her nose, her ears—she was a tough one. She was eighteen years old when she died. It was hurtful, but she lived a good life. After Buffy died, our granddaughter gave my wife, Betty, and me another cat, Peaches, to keep us both company. Betty has since passed away, so now Peaches just keeps me company.

—Charlie Motta

Dixie Memorial Pet Cemetery
Millington, Tennessee

Sissy was ill for a while and my vet said she was in pain. I met with Barbara at Dixie Memorial Pet Cemetery to arrange services several days in advance. I lived with my Sissy longer than I'd lived with anybody, including parents and husband. She made me laugh, smile, and play, even when I felt bad. She was pure joy wrapped up in fur. When she passed, I was totally pain stricken. I felt I had lost the only living thing who truly knew and loved me, and who I loved equally. I loved her as much as any family member, sometimes more. She certainly deserved equal treatment. Burying her in a pet cemetery is the best thing I could do for one I loved so much.

I think preplanning helped a lot with my grief, but I also had another very young pet at home who I could sit and cry with, who didn't think I was nuts. I will always miss Sissy. I visit her several times a year. I believe she's busy in heaven. I waited until my grandmother's birthday (who also passed) to send Sissy to her. They're busy taking care of each other.

—*Linda M. Williams*

Hartsdale Pet Cemetery and Crematory
Hartsdale, New York

San Diego Pet Memorial Park
San Diego, California

AA Sorrento Valley
Pet Cemetery and Crematory
San Diego, California

One day, looking at the ocean and sky I asked God for a challenge. The most difficult part of this job is controlling my emotions. It's not like any other job. I feel like I can help people deal with their grief by just being there for them. We perform individual cremations daily—from baby canaries to small ponies. One young lad brought his small dog whom he planned to euthanize the following day. We went out to look at the burial plots, and I suggested this one or that one. The dog laid down on the one he preferred, as if lying in the casket. So Be It.

—Velma M. Matthews, AA Sorrento Valley Pet Cemetery and Crematory

Hartsdale Pet Cemetery and Crematory
Hartsdale, New York

The Surrey Pet Cemetery and Crematorium
South Godstone, Surrey • England

Craig Road Pet Cemetery, Funeral Home, and Crematoriums
Las Vegas, Nevada

I had my parrot, Perky, since I was five years old. He had so much personality, and I was his favorite. When I was thirteen, my mother died, so my brother and I went to live with her parents in New York State. We had only a couple of possessions left from our childhood, but we had the parrot, and he moved out with me when I was eighteen. My kids also grew up with him. Once we tied one end of some dental floss to Perky's leg and the other end to my five-year-old son's loose tooth, put Perky on his arm, and when he flew away, my son's tooth was pulled out! Perky died when I was thirty-three. He is the one consistent memory of all those years.

—Michelle Malkowski

Saratoga
Pet Cemetery
Wilton, New York

Cedar Hills
Pet Cemetery
Columbia, Tennessee

Madewood Plantation
Alongside Human Cemetery
Napoleonville, Louisiana

Founded in 1947 in the Bay Area, Pet's Rest Cemetery, Crematory for Pet Animals is definitely the most unique cemetery in Colma, San Francisco's necropolis—City of the Dead. Within Colma's approximate 2.5 square miles lie more than fifteen human cemeteries of all denominations. Pet's Rest is said to be the most visited of all the cemeteries. Of the more than 15,000 pets buried there, it's common to see not only memorials for dogs and cats, but also for monkeys, cheetahs, iguanas, snakes, and goldfish, to name a few! Unique and unusual monuments fill the landscape with testaments of devotion. A visit to Pet's Rest is always an adventure in wonderment and awe. It's no surprise that there have been relationships developed between clients that range from friendship and carpooling to love and marriage. One almost never sees interactions in human cemeteries, but here people bring pictures and stories, and share them readily.

—Phillip C'de Baca, Pet's Rest Cemetery, Crematory for Pet Animals

Craig Road Pet Cemetery,
Funeral Home, and Crematoriums
Las Vegas, Nevada

AA Sorrento Valley
Pet Cemetery and Crematory
San Diego, California

Hartsdale Pet Cemetery and Crematory
Hartsdale, New York

Fella: U.S. Marine Corps War Hero

A pet cemetery is one of the last places you might expect to find a war hero. But a World War II war hero is indeed buried at the Oak Lawn Pet Cemetery in Miami-Dade County, a dog named Fella.

Since Fella was laid to rest forty-five years ago, the Humane Society of Greater Miami, which owns the nonprofit cemetery, has flown an American flag over his grave. The headstone reads, U.S. Marine Corps, *and in large letters proclaims,* War Hero. *It says he was born in 1941. According to old news clippings, some time after the war he came with an owner to south Florida, where the dog died in 1954. Old Humane Society articles describe Fella as a "faithful and intelligent dog" who served in the South Pacific, was commended for action at Guadalcanal, and credited with saving many lives. Old friends of the Society remember Fella's special full-dress Marine Corps burial in which he was wrapped in his war jacket decorated with medals.*

Besides his headstone and some news clippings, not much was known about this war hero. The name Wade, *which appears on his headstone, and the dog's breed remained part of the mystery. But all that changed when the* Miami Herald *covered Fella's story on Memorial Day weekend in 1999.*

The story was distributed nationally by the Associated Press and was read by a woman who knew Fella as a child. Kay McCall was born the same year as Fella and grew up next door to his owner, Dave Wade. Surprised and deeply touched by the article, McCall immediately contacted the Humane Society to share Fella's story.

While Wade wasn't Fella's handler during the war, he, like Fella, was a World War II veteran. McCall explained that Wade was so impressed by Fella's intelligence that he talked the military into letting him care for the dog after the war. Fella was Wade's whole life.

McCall described Fella as "gorgeous and smarter than Lassie." A German shepherd and collie mixed breed, Fella had long, featherlike fur on his tail, chest, and legs. Since McCall's mother wouldn't allow her and her sister to have a dog, they quickly took to Fella's kind companionship. While Wade was at work, the girls spent hours playing with Fella. When Fella died, the McCall sisters attended the funeral. Like many others who lose their furry best friends, Kay McCall expressed, "I'll never forget that dog."

The 1999 Miami hurricane destroyed the American flag flown over Fella's grave. In an effort to continue to honor Fella's memory, the Humane Society asked the American Legion to donate a flag to his grave. On December 17, 1999, not only did they donate a flag but the American Legion Color Guard made a personal visit to Fella's grave and conducted a formal presentation of the new American flag, complete with a gun salute. The beautiful ceremony exemplified the power and importance of the human-animal bond and deeply touched all in attendance. Fella's memory will forever live on and be honored.

—Kelly F. Grimm, Oak Lawn Pet Cemetery at the Humane Society of Greater Miami

Paw Print Gardens
Pet Cemetery and Crematory
West Chicago, Illinois

Rolling Acres Pet Cemetery
Troy, New York

In a strange way, the Humane Society of Greater Miami's pet cemetery is a peaceful and happy place for shelter workers to escape to. Every day we come face to face with irresponsible pet owners—people who have either neglected, abused, or who simply find it easy to give away the family pet. At times, it becomes very easy to become angry with mankind and lose faith in our fellow human, but everything is back in perspective when we're in the cemetery. We have a small group of "regulars" who come back time and time again to visit their pets. To walk quietly by the headstones that read, 'My heart lies here' or 'Scruffy, forever my best friend' helps us remember the good in people, the love people have for their pets, and the reason why we come to work every day, fighting to create a more responsible, humane society. Helping those who cannot help themselves—the cats and dogs of our community—is what makes being in this field gratifying."

—Kelly F. Grimm, Oak Lawn Pet Cemetery at the Humane Society of Greater Miami

Craig Road Pet Cemetery,
Funeral Home, and Crematoriums
Las Vegas, Nevada

Pet Heaven
Memorial Park
Miami, Florida

Gypsy
Rest In Peace
Jerome, Arizona

When people are grieving over the loss of a pet, mostly I try to just listen and be a physical presence. It is not uncommon for owners to call back after the initial impact and want to talk more about the death of their pet. Everyone has their own timetable on grieving; you just have to let each person go through it their own way and try to help when you can. It angers me when some people make light about the death of a pet. I have lost animals to various medical problems and it's not easy saying good-bye and letting go. We offer four basic burial options for our clients. The first two involve cremation—with the remains returned, or not. The last two are burial—on the owner's property, if laws permit, or at a pet cemetery. I have many touching stories about my patients; each gives me strength on those difficult days when I feel overwhelmed.

—*Carole Treat, D.V.M.*

Private
Pet Memorial
Fletcher, North Carolina

Private
Pet Memorial
Fletcher, North Carolina

My cat, Claude, used to make everyone in my family laugh with his crazy mannerisms such as catching flies or playing fetch with a Superball. He and I had a wonderful relationship. He would hang out with me in the garden. He acted as though he knew how much I enjoyed being there. It made me smile. I'd pet him and call him my garden kitty. He loved to hunt mice and birds in our backyard and in the field across the street. He was always very proud of his catch of the day.

One day while I was at work, I received the phone call that a white cat had been hit in front of my house and that it may be Claude. My emotions went haywire. I started to cry and left work immediately. By the time I got home, the girls next door were already burying Claude's body in the field across the street. They said I wouldn't want to see him, so I decided to go back to the house.

When I visited Claude's grave, I brought fresh flowers from our garden. This helped me get through a lot of my grief. It felt good to cry. I thought about relocating him to our backyard, but then I felt he would be at peace in what was once his favorite place to run free. A few months later, I went back to visit his grave. The field was overgrown, so I had a hard time finding it. When I finally found it, I couldn't believe my eyes. It had been dug up, and I saw tufts of white fur leading off into the open field.

There are times when I look across the street into the field and my eyes well up with tears. It really was not my decision to bury Claude in the field across the street. My preference would have been to bury him in our backyard, so my children could visit his grave too. But now that I don't have a grave to visit, I have set up a little memorial for Claude in the house. This seems to help everyone in the family. Sometimes I daydream that he's sitting in his favorite spot right next to me. Claude was a special cat with a wonderful personality. My family and I will never forget our special Claudie Boy.

—Mary Ann Beals

The Surrey Pet Cemetery and Crematorium

South Godstone, Surrey • England

Dixie Memorial Pet Cemetery

Millington, Tennessee

San Diego Pet Memorial Park
San Diego, California

Rolling Acres Pet Cemetery
Troy, New York

The Last Battle

Pet Heaven
Memorial Park
Miami, Florida

If it should be that I grow frail and weak,
And pain should keep me from my sleep,
Then will you do what must be done,
For this—the last battle—can't be won.
You will be sad, I understand.
But don't let grief then stay your hand,
For on this day, more than the rest,
Your love and friendship must stand the test.
We have had so many happy years,
You wouldn't want me to suffer so.
When the time comes, please let me go.
Take me to where my needs they'll tend,
Only, stay with me until the end.
And hold me firm and speak to me,
Until my eyes no longer see.
I know in time you will agree,
It is a kindness you do to me.
Although my tail its last has waved,
From pain and suffering I have been saved.
Don't grieve that it must be you,
Who has to decide this thing to do.
We've been so close—we two—these years,
Don't let your heart hold any tears.

—Anonymous

Rolling Acres
Pet Cemetery
Troy, New York

Divine intervention prompted me to get involved in the pet cemetery business. I have found my niche in life, and I am at peace. No part of this job is difficult as long as my heart remains involved. Listening, listening, listening is how I help people deal with their grief.

—Darla Norrish, The Pet Cemetery of Tucson

Pet Heaven
Memorial Park
Miami, Florida

Bubbling Well
Pet Memorial Park
Napa, California

Paw Print Gardens
Pet Cemetery and Crematory
West Chicago, Illinois

I have always had two or three pets. Right now, I have two cats and two dogs. I cannot say my pets have gone into grieving over each other. Maybe it's because at the loss of one, we cling to the living pets. I still feel the presence of my deceased pets. Maybe it's because that is the window my cat looked out of, this is my dog's favorite chair. Beautiful memories never seem to fade away. When remembering my animal friends, I think of the gentleness, the devotion, the true dedication, and mostly the unconditional love that surpasses all human understanding. That little paw that stroked my cheek, that tongue that licked away my tears when I was upset, that tail that almost wagged itself off when I came home, that uncanny knowledge of when I was hurt or upset, that warning bark when a stranger was near. Oh, I could go on and on, but I will not. Our pets are just wonderful. They deserve the best burial possible. Nothing could repay what they give us; no amount of money can buy that kind of love.

—Patricia Blosser, Paw Print Gardens Pet Cemetery and Crematory

AA Sorrento Valley
Pet Cemetery and Crematory
San Diego, California

Hartsdale Pet Cemetery
and Crematory
Hartsdale, New York

Rolling Acres
Pet Cemetery
Troy, New York

My heart was broken. I had lost my best friend. He was always there for me. When I was sick, he would lie by me. When my parents came in to check on me, he would put his paws on me. I decided to bury him in a pet cemetery because I always want to have access to him. The fact that my Baby was in a place where I could go and visit him is what helped me through my grief. When I look at pictures and go to sit and talk to him, I do feel a sense of him being present. Our other cat may have felt the loss: he seemed to know he could do things differently.

—Penny Blais

Private
Pet Memorial
Weaverville, North Carolina

Dixie Memorial
Pet Cemetery
Millington, Tennessee

If the death was not a sudden or unexpected one, we would have a lined casket ready, with special pictures and toys picked out to go into it. We chose the pet cemetery as the final resting place because I needed a place where I could feel close to my pets. Before my husband passed away, we always went to the cemetery on special days: their birthdays, the anniversary of their deaths, even Mother's Day because one was a mother. A few weeks before Christmas, we would decorate a tree with battery operated lights, and place a red rose in a watering tube for each grave to signify love. For Easter, it would be an egg tree.

Our second dog had spinal cancer and couldn't walk. We kept five of her offspring, plus her granddaughter. The morning she was to be put to sleep, we gave her a little individual time with each of them. She was such a good mother. I always experienced a deep sense of loss with each pet's passing because each animal is unique—I cared for each one differently, and I miss that uniqueness. For instance, I just lost my Becky. For years I would hold her bowl in my lap at mealtime to slow her down. What a void that has left. She would drool on the front of my cupboards while I was fixing the food bowls. Now there is no more drool to wipe up. I will never forget her. I never had children. I always felt my pets were my babies—kissing them a lot, and telling them how beautiful they were.

I remember our first bitch and all the beautiful pups she gave us, the obedience training my late husband did with three of the dogs and the joy of coming home from a dog show with a ribbon or trophy. I remember the puppy years and the chewed furniture, cupboards, windowsills, shoes. But most of all, I remember the love they gave.

—Phyllis Christian

Saratoga
Pet Cemetery
Wilton, New York

Hartsdale Pet Cemetery
and Crematory
Hartsdale, New York

The Surrey Pet Cemetery
and Crematorium

South Godstone, Surrey • England

Pet Heaven
Memorial Park

Miami, Florida

Dina Simone
Private Memorial
Palm Coast, Florida

Dina

As we lay you down to eternal rest,
We ask ourselves, "Did we do our best?"
You were more than just a pet—
Our life,
Our love,
Our friend.

God has called upon you on this day;
We answer Him with your soul, but please
Not to stray.
As you stand beside Him at the gate,
Please believe us, there is no hate, only
Fate and love that you deserve.
As we say good-bye, we will not cry
You'll always be that sparkle in our eyes.
We all love you dearly.
We did our best, so that you may have a
Peaceful Rest

Always in our hearts, until we meet again,
Love,

—Your family, John, Barbara and Michelle Simone
and your soulmate Max

In 1896, a prominent New York City veterinarian Dr. Samuel Johnson offered his apple orchard in then-rural Hartsdale, New York, to serve as a burial plot for a bereaved friend's dog. That single compassionate act served as the cornerstone for what was to become America's first and most prestigious pet cemetery.

Today, continuing a long history of caring and excellence, this beautiful hillside location, known to many as The Peaceable Kingdom in Hartsdale, is the final resting place for nearly 70,000 pets. Dogs, cats, birds, reptiles, monkeys, and even a lion cub, are among those buried at the Hartsdale cemetery. Regardless of the species, the common thread is that all were special and loved. Generations of pet owners have embraced these pet animals and made them part of their families. We understand the profound sense of loss that one feels when a pet dies.

While we cannot bring your pet back, our objective simply is to make you feel a little better at a time of loss and sorrow. From the time we are contacted we spare no detail to lessen the burden of your grief. We make all the necessary arrangements to transport your pet either from your home or your veterinarian's office. We encourage pet owners to visit the cemetery in advance and plan every detail so they can be certain that their pets will receive the kind of final tribute they wish. Prior to burial, pet owners may spend a final moment of peace and solitude with their pet in our private viewing room, and then they may witness the burial at the gravesite if desired.

Never forgotten, the hero canines of war are honored every Memorial Day. A tradition that began years ago when a man known only as Arthur came every year to lay a wreath at the War Dog Memorial. For reasons unknown, this veteran of the Battle of the Bulge was no longer able to come. In 1981, continuous remembrance was assured when Commander Thaddeus Ogden passed a special resolution to the bylaws of his post stating that a wreath, a firing detail, and services would be furnished on Memorial Day, forever. Hundreds of people now attend these heartfelt services every year.

—Edward C. Martin, Jr., Hartsdale Pet Cemetery and Crematory

Hartsdale Pet Cemetery
and Crematory
Hartsdale, New York

Hartsdale Pet Cemetery
and Crematory
Hartsdale, New York

Bubbling Well
Pet Memorial Park
Napa, California

Craig Road Pet Cemetery,
Funeral Home, and Crematoriums
Las Vegas, Nevada

Poem for Grieving

Paw Print Gardens
Pet Cemetery and Crematory
West Chicago, Illinois

Do not stand at my grave and weep.
I am not there, I do not sleep.
I am a thousand winds that blow,
I am the diamond glints on snow.
I am the sunlight on ripened grain,
I am the gentle autumn's rain.
When you awake in the morning's hush,
I am the swift uplifting rush
Of quiet birds in circled flight.
I am the stars that shine at night.
Do not stand at my grave and cry,
I am not there, I did not die.

—Anonymous

Broward Pet Cemetery and Crematory
Plantation, Florida

We had our cat, Rocky, for just a little while before we discovered he had a hole in his heart and could pass away at any time. We decided to keep him and give him the best life possible. We spoiled him terribly and gave him anything he wanted, including my cashmere scarf to sleep on. He died when he was fifteen months old. We feel that it was a privilege to have had him in our lives. We sadly but lovingly buried him in our flower garden in our backyard. Every time I weed or plant a new annual, I remember him.

—Yvette M. Alexopoulos

Dixie Memorial
Pet Cemetery
Millington, Tennessee

The Surrey Pet Cemetery
and Crematorium
South Godstone, Surrey • England

Pet Heaven
Memorial Park
Miami, Florida

With a Smile

Toby was nineteen. *Last year I thought he was on his last legs. He used to weigh 12 pounds, but by last year he weighed 7. He had stopped eating and my vet was preparing me for making the "big decision." I just didn't feel as though Toby was done living. I took him home and* *force-fed him for about a week. We spent evenings in front of the fire, which he loved. I bought him a heated bed. Suddenly, Toby began eating again.*

In the past year, Toby had gained maybe a pound or two. Although he was just hanging on to life, he still purred, walked outside to bask in the sun, hung around our active dogs, and was truly enjoying himself despite his frailty. I knew he wouldn't be with us for much longer.

I can't help thinking about all the time we had spent together. Toby used to go on walks with my dog and me. He always greeted me at the door when I came home and had always unashamedly demanded attention and affection from people. In his younger days, Toby thought it was great fun to hide in the long grass in our front yard and leap out at unsuspecting dogs as they and their people strolled down the sidewalk. Once he saved me from a possible fire by waking me up in the middle of the night when the neighbor's house was ablaze. I knew Toby was special when my brother was in the hospital suffering from a concussion after a car accident and all he could say was, Here Toby kitty kitty *over and over again. My brother had spent years claiming he didn't like Toby at all.*

Toby had always been a happy-go-lucky cat. That's probably one reason he lived for so long. He had been with me for nearly half my life—longer than most of my friends and longer than I've known my husband. His age or cancer or some other malady finally took him. But even at the end, when he weighed a mere 3.4 pounds and could hardly hold his head up, Toby tried to be in the middle of all the action of the household. Even at the end he was demanding affection.

I want to keep Toby near me, so I had him cremated. He sits in a high, warm spot in my house in an urn I've chosen especially for him. Every once in a while, my dog stops in his tracks and points his nose upward at the spot where Toby is. Does he know? It was rough when it was finally time for Toby to go, but I will always smile when I think of him.

—Ruth Berman

We knew that someday we would have to face the loss of our pets and did not want to make arrangements under emotional stress. After seeing a special on pet cemeteries on TV, we decided to bury our pets when the time came.

Our pets were our children. When they passed, we felt a tremendous loss. Our home was empty. There was no one to greet us at the door or play with us after a tough day. Our belief in God, our hope that they are in a better place, and the knowledge that they are not suffering is what has helped us through our grief. We visit them about once a month during the warm weather, and once or twice during the winter. The cemetery is a peaceful place and well taken care of.

We had Misty and MacDougall at the same time. Misty liked to lie next to me. MacDougall was my little boy, and my protector. When Misty passed, MacDougall would look for her around the house and yard. Holly liked to lay in my arms on her back, like a baby, and hog our queen-size bed. It feels like she is still here. At times it seems like I see a glimpse of a shadow going into our bedroom.

—Deborah Graulty

The Surrey Pet Cemetery
and Crematorium

South Godstone, Surrey • England

Hyde Park
Pet Cemetery

London • England

San Diego Pet Memorial Park
San Diego, California

On many occasions I find a stick placed on this one particular memorial. Each time the pet owners visit their beloved Labrador, they leave a fetch stick to let her know they were there to visit and to reminisce about her wonderful love to retrieve. A little squirrel adorns the monument to Nickie, who lived to give chase to the squirrels in her yard. Sea shells are left to grace the memory of Buffy, a Pekingese who obviously loved to walk the beach.

—James L. Boles, Jr., Good Shepherd Pet Crematory and Cemetery

Craig Road Pet Cemetery,
Funeral Home, and Crematoriums
Las Vegas, Nevada

Paw Print Gardens
Pet Cemetery and Crematory
West Chicago, Illinois

Bubbling Well
Pet Memorial Park
Napa, California

Excerpted from

Simply Precious: Moments in Time with a Remarkable Cat

by Muriel L. Hine

Her love for children is eminent. I'm sure her original home had children. Our neighbors never had to look far for their kids. They were always in our yard playing with Precious.

One of the cat's little playmates was diagnosed with a tumor and was sent to a children's hospital in New England. We went to visit him. We thought we would have to leave Precious at the motel, but the hospital welcomed pets. Many youngsters were terminally ill, but all were excited when we arrived. Children romped in the recreation area. Precious modeled clothes, rode in a wagon, and knocked down blocks. Patients confined to bed received special visits.

After an afternoon at the hospital, we returned to our motel. Precious was restless. Muriel and I knew something was going on, mentally, with this cat.

"I'll take her for a walk," Muriel said and put the blue harness on the cat. Precious pulled at her leash. "Calm down," Muriel told her four-legged friend. "We both need some air."

"I'll wait for you in the lobby. My legs have just about had it for today," I told Muriel. The desk clerk saw Muriel and Precious leave the building. The telephone rang. The young lady behind the desk called to me. "Precious has a phone call."

"What?" I answered as I started across the room.

"Precious has a phone call," she repeated. "It sounds urgent."

In the excitement, the hospital attendant had forgotten my name but knew the name of my four-legged companion. Kevin Babcock, a critically ill patient, had taken a turn for the worse and had asked for Precious. An eerie feeling enveloped me once more. Precious knew something was wrong.

Kevin smiled when we walked into his room. Precious went to his outstretched arms and snuggled down, resting her head next to his chin. For over an hour, the boy stroked her back while she looked into his face, purring her contentment. The strokes stopped. The small thin hand went limp. Precious nudged Kevin's hand but it didn't move. Her head pushed his hand again. It still didn't move.

She glanced our way, gave the boy a nudge with her head, wiggled from his body and came to me. She knew her special friend was gone. Kevin's mother went to the boy's bed. We stood outside the hospital room door to allow Mrs. Babcock some privacy in her initial moments of grief. Choked with emotion, Kevin's mother approached us.

"Kevin talked of nothing but Precious these past two days. Thank you for making his last moments such happy ones."

Precious was quiet. Her body trembled. Mrs. Babcock scratched my companion's ears, adding, "This little girl is simply precious." Muriel and I burst into tears. A young woman had just lost her son, yet she was thanking Precious for being there. The cat was a comfort to a stranger, even in death.

❤ ❤ ❤

We prepared for Precious's death in advance. She had been ill and winter was coming on, so we wanted to be sure there was a place for her should she leave us. She pulled through that terrible ordeal and lived two more years. The fact that Precious again became ill made it easier for me to say good-bye. I didn't want her to suffer. To be honest, I don't think I'll ever get over losing her. She left such a great legacy that I'm constantly reminded of what a remarkable little girl she was.

I think those who are close to their pets, as I was to Precious, can describe their loss as being like losing a family member. In fact, friends commented that we took the death of Precious harder than

Precious's
Final Resting Place
Wilton, New York

two members of my immediate family. My response was, "That's because Precious did more for me than those members of my family. She was always there for me." I can't truthfully say I'm through the grief of having lost my best friend.

I originally thought Precious would be buried in our little pet cemetery in our backyard. When she became a celebrity, however, I felt she should have a more dignified resting place. I'm glad I made that decision because so many people have visited her grave and left flowers. I visit her grave during the nice weather. Take flowers, have a prayer. After Thanksgiving, I go to put something on her grave for Christmas and return when the snow is gone. I feel Precious's presence all the time. I know she's still with me in spirit.

I had home burial services in my neighborhood from the time I was twelve years old, and as a young man, I was employed at a funeral home for humans. Today, at my pet cemetery, I offer the same services that a human funeral home, cemetery, and crematory offer, including embalming, funeral services, and perpetual care.

The most difficult part of my job is knowing the heartbreak people feel when their pets have reached the end of their lives. By being here, talking with them, offering services of comfort, and providing poems, pet loss books, and grief counselors when needed, I am doing what I can to help people deal with their feelings of loss.

Over and over clients describe how their pets have helped them through tough times in their personal lives. Many of the pets were taken in as strays and had become wonderful members of the family. The pets seemed grateful for their rescue. There was an unspoken bond: You saved my life.

—Doyle Shugart, Deceased Pet Care Funeral Home and Crematory, Loving Care Pet Cemetery, and Oak Rest Pet Gardens Funeral Home and Crematory

Rolling Acres
Pet Cemetery
Troy, New York

AA Sorrento Valley
Pet Cemetery and Crematory
San Diego, California

Craig Road Pet Cemetery,
Funeral Home, and Crematoriums
Las Vegas, Nevada

Adapted from The Las Vegas Sun, *April 1999*

"Beloved Duke Leaves Behind Cherished Memories at Cemetery"

by David Clayton

People passing by Old Duke wave, nod, or smile in returning his greeting, which is spiritual now but warm, compassionate, and faithful as ever. His heart-shaped memorial, with the word Greeter *permanently etched into its base, stands in the Eternal Garden of Peace, near the door to the office of the Craig Road Pet Cemetery. The thousands of people who came to know Duke over the past thirteen years can still feel his presence and sense the earnest offer of sympathy and companionship he extended to all grieving families.*

Old Duke, a yellow Lab and bull terrier mix, died in his sleep on March 30, 1999, but only after putting in another full day at the job he invented. Burying a beloved pet can be nearly as emotional as burying a human family member. No one knew this more than Duke, who sensed the proper decorum as he attended funerals and greeted visiting families. If the family wanted to relieve the stress with play, Duke was there to fetch stones for as long as they would throw them. If they wanted quiet, he understood. If they needed a furry head to pat, his was always there.

He took his responsibilities so seriously that he would greet visitors in the cemetery's parking lot and escort them right to their pets' gravesites. He would often do this while walking ahead of them, stopping at the exact headstone before turning his eyes upward and then taking an appropriate few steps backward to give the family room. This astonishing but marvelous feat comforted families of the almost 4,200 animals at rest there, and made Duke a legend among them.

Saying good-bye is something owner Tony Clayton is still dealing with, particularly in the mornings. Duke would jump out of Clayton's pickup and start his day by running through the whole cemetery, sniffing out all the dog biscuits people would leave at the grave sites. Then he would position himself outside the office door, a good spot for seeing visitors as they pulled in.

"This was a dog that was put on earth to do something, and by God he did for thirteen years," Clayton said. "He put families at ease, comforting them in their loss."

Broward Pet Cemetery and Crematory
Plantation, Florida

When our Dobermans Shanea and Megan first passed, it was devastating and overwhelming. They had been part of our lives—our family. But we were able to visit them daily because they were buried in caskets in our backyard. When we put our house up for sale, however, we decided to move the dogs to a pet cemetery because we still wanted to be able to visit them. The owners of the cemetery compassionately and professionally handled the removal of the caskets from our backyard to interment at their location. Shanea and Megan have been gone for a while now, so we do not feel their presence as we did at first. We are comforted knowing that they are having a good time up in "doggie heaven," and that one day we will join them so we can all be together again.

— Lois A. Rohloff and Barbara A. Van Deusen

Pet Heaven
Memorial Park
Miami, Florida

Rolling Acres
Pet Cemetery
Troy, New York

Hartsdale Pet Cemetery and Crematory
Hartsdale, New York

Grace had the gentlest black eyes I have ever seen in a Labrador. She had a way of looking at me and conveying her feelings of trust and unconditional love. Being with her during the euthanasia process allowed me to hold her while she comfortably fell into a deep sleep without pain. It allowed me to let her know she was safe in my arms until the very end.

I had supportive friends who shared my grief, and my ten-year-old Lab, Beretta, who was there for me too. We went through the grieving process together. When the time was right, I moved Gracie to a special part of my heart and was able to get another puppy. It took several weeks for a relationship to develop between the new puppy and Beretta, but when it happened, it brought new life and love back to us all.

— Jacklyn B. Coger

Paw Print Gardens
Pet Cemetery and Crematory
West Chicago, Illinois

Hyde Park
Pet Cemetery
London • England

Craig Road Pet Cemetery, Funeral Home, and Crematoriums
Las Vegas, Nevada

I have always prepared for my pets' departure in advance because I want them safe, buried with love and dignity in a place where I can visit and remember the good times we have had together. I still grieve and reminisce over my sweet pets. You see, in my sixty-seven years I've lost at least ten beloved pets. I still have my beloved Sheltie, Mr. Higgins, and Binki, my cat. Before losing a pet, I had another one chosen for me, by my pet. Who else could choose the right one? That pet also helped the new one adjust to me. This was the greatest blessing. This was love. Each pet has taught me a different thing about life. Put together, I learned about unconditional love, caring, and wisdom, not to take myself too seriously, to trust in God completely, to always look for a rainbow, and that we are really never alone. I still feel their presence in my home, and I visit their graves often. Spring. Summer. Fall. Pet Memorial Day in September to plant mums. Every Christmas. I visit them at least once a month to make sure there are flowers and to honor them. You see, I still love each one.

—Rena Edwards

Saratoga
Pet Cemetery
Wilton, New York

San Diego Pet
Memorial Park
San Diego, California

Hartsdale Pet Cemetery and Crematory

Hartsdale, New York

Paw Print Gardens Pet Cemetery and Crematory

West Chicago, Illinois

Remembering

Dixie Memorial
Pet Cemetery
Millington, Tennessee

We threw away the wicker bed
And gave away the ball.
We gathered up the leather leash,
Then kept it after all.

Old dog was much too weary—
Too hurt to run about.
He did not rise that morning.
His exhausted heart gave out.

His eyes were closed forever
And his wagging tail was still.
Softly, softly in the springtime,
He was buried on the hill.

Yet there still are times we see him,
Springing toward us on the lawn.
But if we kneel to call him to us,
Like a shadow he is gone.

—Anonymous

Cedar Hills Pet Cemetery
Columbia, Tennessee

Arlo,
the K-9 Hero

Arlo served with me *as an Oklahoma City Police K-9 from 1990 to 1997. He enjoyed police work and was talented in narcotic and cadaver detection, in addition to his patrol duties. He was successful in the apprehension of numerous felony suspects and protected officers from injury due to violent, unruly crowds on many occasions. When detecting narcotics or searching for a deceased person, Arlo completed his tasks, knowing that if successful he would be allowed to play with a rubber ball. Being allowed to play with his ball gave him the drive and incentive to work.*

At home, Arlo was a member of my family and was bonded with my wife and daughters. He had such an attachment to my youngest daughter that I could not discipline her in front of him. If I raised my voice toward her in any way, Arlo would put me on notice that he did not like it. When I was away from home, I knew my family was well protected as long as Arlo was there.

Most police dogs are proud animals who do not get along with one another, but Arlo was an exception. He was a team player. He bonded with and really liked another police K-9 named Gunny, and the two of them together made history in the rescue recovery effort at the Alfred P. Murrah Federal Building bombing in Oklahoma City. Arlo and Gunny worked the bombsite from the beginning on April 19, 1995.

On May 3, the Federal Emergency Management Agency teams were going home while twenty-three victims remained in the building unaccounted for. The medical examiner notified Don Browning, who was Gunny's handler, and requested our assistance in recovering these remaining victims.

We entered the bombsite with both dogs. The dogs worked together with Arlo indicating the location of a victim and Gunny confirming it, or with Gunny finding a victim and Arlo confirming the find. Both dogs located twenty victims buried in the rubble. They also detected the locations of the three remaining victims whose bodies could not be recovered until after the building's implosion on May 13. On May 29, Gunny and Arlo returned to the site and once again found these three victims.

I retired Arlo from active service in July 1997. I attempted to work with a new K-9, but it just didn't work out. My heart belonged to Arlo, so I too got out of K-9 work and returned to the role of patrol officer.

In July 1999, Arlo, whom I got to keep after retirement, became ill with cancer. I had made the dreaded decision to have him put to sleep to ease his suffering. On July 5, I went out to the backyard to take him to the vet to be euthanized. Arlo walked over to me. I leaned down to hug him and hook on his leash. Once more, Arlo took charge and spared me the task of ending his life. He laid his head on my lap, took a deep breath, released his spirit, and died in my arms. Arlo was buried with full police honors and with a proclamation from the Governor of Oklahoma. The good people at Precious Pets Cemetery provided the services for him.

Arlo taught me many things. The most important was that these wonderful creatures are gifts from God to man and then are called home just as we humans are. He was my partner, my friend, and a member of my family. I love him very much and he will always occupy a place in my heart.

—Sgt. Ron Burks, Oklahoma City Police Department

❤ ❤ ❤

The Governor proclaimed July 5, 1999, Sgt. Maj. Arlo Day. It was a peaceful morning. Bagpipes chanted a mournful tune. Uniformed policemen cried. A four-man honor guard carried the casket. The chaplain told the crowd of the great hero. This was the setting for the funeral of Sgt. Maj. Arlo, a German shepherd who had been a member of the Oklahoma City Police Department's K-9 Unit. He had retired after serving eight years with his handler, Sgt. Ron Burks. Arlo was buried at Precious Pets Cemetery in Spencer, Oklahoma.

Arlo was no ordinary dog. Arlo (with another Oklahoma City K-9, Gunny) had recovered twenty-three victims from the Alfred P. Murrah Federal Building's rubble after the bombing in 1995. The dogs worked around the clock for the last two days of the recovery and found twenty bodies. They found the remaining three bodies after the building's implosion.

Most animals buried at the Precious Pets Cemetery receive a funeral, and most police dogs receive a special funeral. But to the people of Oklahoma who had watched with horror and dismay the days and weeks of rescue efforts following the bombing, Arlo's funeral was not only special but necessary. Among the many people attending was a lady who had brought flowers and through her tears thanked Arlo for finding her friend's body weeks after the bombing. Representatives from the Archives for the Oklahoma City National Memorial attended the funeral to complete Arlo's story.

In the end, Arlo had been crippled with arthritis and cancer. His owner and former partner, Sgt. Burks, made arrangements with the veterinarian and cemetery to have the dog euthanized and buried. When Burks went outside to tell Arlo of his decision, the dog hobbled over to him, put his head in his lap, and died. Relieving Sgt. Burks of the task of euthanasia was Arlo's final gift of love.

The Precious Pets Cemetery has a special garden, called Faithful Guardians, dedicated to police dogs. Five other police dogs, Trux, Dandy, Bo, Chita, and Ben, who worked at the Murrah Federal Building after the bombing are buried there. When it is Gunny's time, he, too, will be buried beside his friend and coworker, Arlo.

—Linda McCullough, Precious Pets Cemetery and Crematory

Helping clients through the grieving process is one of the most important roles we provide. To best meet this need we work in conjunction with a certified psychologist who currently runs the San Diego Pet Bereavement Group. We are a yearly stop for at least three local colleges wanting to educate those going into the field of animal medicine on how to respond to clients before and after a pet has been euthanized.

The most difficult part of our job is seeing the pain in pet owners who had a unique bond with their pet. By unique, I do not mean to imply that these individuals care more for their pets than you or I do. I mean that their bond was different in a way that does not allow them to go through the initial stages of the grieving process for one reason or another. These individuals are virtually locked into a prison of that initial pain and are truly and utterly wrecked by the loss, which is one of the reasons we initiated the Pet Loss Support Group Program. The program is a huge success, and knowing these people will soon be at peace with their loss makes one of the harder parts of our job a little easier.

The love seen here is tremendous. The stories are endless—from heroic pets actually saving lives, to those of pure devotion till the end. No one story could do justice to them all. I can say that although the stories I hear may be beautiful, scary, exciting, funny, or sad, all of them are told with love and illustrate the loving bond between pets and their people.

—Patrick Jay Brady, San Diego Pet Memorial Park

San Diego Pet Memorial Park
San Diego, California

San Diego Pet Memorial Park
San Diego, California

"He was my best friend."

"She was always by my side."

"He was like my child."

"She was pure love wrapped in fur."

"He was so smart, I swear he was human."

"She had the best personality . . . gentle, kind, funny . . . "

"I loved him more than some of my family members."

"She deserved the best send-off I could possibly give."

"His death was devastating to me. I will never get over it."

For nearly two years, these words were repeated to me like mantras. I heard them over and over. Whether I was speaking with someone on the phone who had suffered the loss of an animal companion, whether I was talking with a pet cemeterian at his or her location, whether I was reading epitaphs carved into gravestones or handwritten statements sent to me by mail, these words chanted in my head. There was no doubt in my mind that the bond that humans and animals form is intensely powerful. I knew I was doing the right thing by creating this book. I owed it to the people who shared stories with me. I owed it to the loyal creatures we call pets.

My travels took me to places I would never have been able to visualize. In public places for all the world to see, I witnessed elaborate displays of dedication from people to their animal friends. I felt the pain in beautitul little memorials set up on private properties or in people's homes to commemorate their deceased companion. It was difficult to hold back tears when experiencing all of this raw, honest emotion, but it was easy to feel the large spirit of these tiny, furry, feathered, scaly beings.

This spirit is what guided me.

That energy is what fueled me.

This book is the result.

Your feelings are the proof.

My First Experience.
Craig Road Pet Cemetery,
Funeral Home, and Crematoriums
Las Vegas, Nevada

Leeds Castle
Trees Near Dog Graves
Maidstone, Kent • England

You have a choice.

The death of a pet is a sad and trying time for most people. If you wait until your pet dies to make final arrangements, you may cause yourself further emotional stress and make decisions you will later regret. There are many ways to lay a pet to rest, and because of these many options and the emotions involved, it is wise to prepare for your pet's death in advance.

If you have not made final arrangements before your pet dies, don't panic. There is no need to rush into a decision. If your pet dies at home, find the coldest part of your dwelling, such as the basement floor, garage floor, an enclosed porch, or the trunk of your car, until decisions and preparations can be made. First, lay down a piece of plastic and place a newspaper or blanket on top of that. Then, lay your pet directly on top of the blanket, and cover him with another blanket, towel, or sheet. Most veterinary clinics or hospitals have cold storage, where your pet can be kept for a day or two, and where you can view his body one last time. Remember, your pet belongs to you. It's your responsibility to decide what is to be done.

Before deciding to bury your pet in your own backyard, check your city and state regulations. If the laws in your region allow for home burials, keep in mind that your pet should be buried in an airtight container deep enough to discourage predators. Never try cremation on your own. If laws do not allow for you to bury your pet in your backyard, you may want to consider a traditional pet cemetery.

Traditional pet cemeteries allow burial sites with upright, above ground memorial markers, slants, tablets, monoliths, or tombstones, which usually require a concrete foundation for support. Flat, ground-level markers, such as those found in memorial parks, and cremation are usually available as well.

Most facilities have selection rooms, where people can choose from a large variety of basic to deluxe caskets, urns, markers, name plates, medallions, photo plaques, figurines, and other types of memorials. Caskets for pets come in all shapes and sizes and are built from a wide variety of materials, ranging from airtight, double-walled, styrene plastic lined with satin to tongue-and-groove solid wood cushioned with pillows to top-of-the-line copper or bronze with hinged lids lined with velvet interiors. They are not much different from those used for people. Pendants or charms, which are a lot like lockets, are available from most cemeteries and are a nice way to hold a small portion of your pet's cremains or lock of fur. These sometimes come in the shape of a heart, cross, or simple vessel, which can be worn on a chain or cord around your neck or displayed in your home.

Paw Print Gardens
Pet Cemetery and Crematory
West Chicago, Illinois

Many pet cemeteries offer preburial services such as embalming and private viewing. Embalming is a process that preserves the body so it can be available for a funeral. It is useful in cases where a body is to be held for a long time, but it is not required for cremation. Freezing can accomplish some of the benefits of embalming. Private viewing in chapels or slumber rooms is a service similar to that which is offered for humans, such as a wake or funeral. Viewing helps a lot of people adjust to the trauma of losing an animal companion. Most locations charge an additional fee for this service. Burial costs vary depending on the method and whether the burial is individual or communal. A maintenance fee is sometimes requested by the pet cemetery for grounds care. Other factors to consider are the type of casket and size of the animal.

Individual burial is the process by which a pet is prepared and buried in a single lot with its own memorial marker. There are many variations from cemetery to cemetery, depending on geographic location, local regulations, available facilities, and range of services.

Communal, or country, burial is looked upon as a more humane while still affordable choice to less desirable forms of pet disposal such as dumping and rendering. The remains or cremains of your pet are interred, or placed into a grave, with those of other pets and then covered with earth. It usually does not include a viewing, casket, urn, or marker. Some communal burials are marked with a memorial wall on which plaques are displayed remembering the deceased pets. Rock gardens, flower beds, ponds, or fountains may be created by pet cemeteries to fulfill the same purpose as memorial walls.

A mausoleum is an above ground structure containing a group of crypts, which are designed to hold remains that have been placed in a casket. This is usually an expensive method of interment and is not available in every pet cemetery.

If you choose to cremate your pet, you're choosing an ancient practice that dates back to the Stone Age. Returning our little friends to ashes is a preferred alternative for many pet owners. Some pet cemeteries are now using cremators—the machine in which cremation takes place—that are similar to the type used for humans. The animal remains are exposed to heat and flame, reduced within minutes to skeletal form, and finally processed to small bone fragments commonly called cremains. A casket is not required for cremation, but if one is used, it must be biodegradable.

Individual cremation is the process by which the cremator is used for the sole purpose of cremating one pet's body at a time. Typically, this is the most expensive form of cremation. Communal cremation is the process by which several deceased pets are placed in the cremator at the same time. When the cycle is complete, the cremains are comingled, and scattered or deposited in a shared location. Private cremation is the process by which the cremator is used for the purpose of cremating more than one pet's body at a time. Each body is placed on a separate stainless steel tray and put into the cremator. There may be three to six other trays in the machine at the same time, but they are not touching—each body is contained in its own privately labeled tray. This system allows the cremains to be processed and remain identified all the way through to completion.

Each deceased pet is given an ID tag upon receipt at the cemetery or crematory. This ID tag stays with the pet from the time the body is received until the cremains are returned to the owner. During the cremation process, the ID tag is placed just outside the cremator. The tag is held by a magnetic clip positioned in a diagram that coincides with the slots or trays inside the machine, allowing positive identification by the machine's operator at all times. Most crematories issue a cremation certificate verifying that the pet was cremated at their facility on a given date.

You still have choices to make once your pet has been cremated. You can choose to keep your pet's cremains in an urn. Urns can vary from simple traditional boxes to elaborate animal figurines, using a variety of materials such as wood, polyester resin, clay, ceramic, marble, granite, polished bronze, and pewter for the temporary or permanent containment of cremains. Most cemeteries display a variety of styles or allow you to special order an urn from catalogs. Engraved nameplates, etched photographs, and other forms of personalized inscriptions are available.

Hartsdale Pet Cemetery and Crematory
Hartsdale, New York

You can keep an urn with you in your home, or at the pet cemetery in a columbarium, which is an arrangement of niches erected for the sole purpose of accepting cremains. A niche is a recessed compartment that is usually sealed with a protective front such as bronze, granite, marble, wood, or glass.

A cremation, or scatter, garden is a special section of land that is set aside for the burial or scattering of cremains. There are also services that scatter cremains out to sea or over mountains, lakes, or other sentimental places. Most areas have no restrictions, but contact your local authorities if you're in doubt.

Alternate methods of disposition are available for pets in some areas of the U.S. Taxidermy is a relatively expensive process that requires the animal's skin and fur to be removed and wrapped on a form or stuffed to recreate it's original lifelike appearance. Freeze-drying is another method that is achieved by removing moisture from the body and leaving the pet intact. Some individuals have gone so far as to use a cryogenic service, where the deceased pet is placed in liquid nitrogen with the hopes of reviving him someday in the future if a cure is found for his terminal illness.

You may want to participate in Pet Memorial Day, which is observed and celebrated by most pet cemeteries on the second Sunday in September. Properly mannered and restrained pets are invited to attend, and sometimes a deceased pet in its urn is in attendance. Most often a minister or priest is available to bless the animals. No matter how you choose to lay your pet to rest or whether you participate in such events as Pet Memorial Day, being well informed about all your options will make your decision easier and your recovery from grief a bit swifter.

Bubbling Well
Pet Memorial Park
Napa, California

Helpful Organizations

PET LOSS GRIEF SUPPORT HOT LINES

For many of these hotlines you must leave a message and your call will be returned. Hours vary. Most hotlines hold you responsible for long-distance charges, and some will call you back collect.

Chicago Veterinary Medical Association (630) 603-3994
Colorado State University, Fort Collins (970) 491-1242
Cornell University, Ithica, NY (607) 253-3932
Iowa State University, Ames (888) 478-7574
Michigan State University, East Lansing (517) 432-2696
Ohio State University, Columbus (614) 292-1823
Tufts University School of Veterinary Medicine, North Grafton, MA (508) 839-7966
University of California, Davis (530) 752-4200
University of Florida, Gainsville (352) 392-4700 ext. 4080
University of Illinois, Urbana (217) 244-2273
University of Pennsylvania, Philadelphia (215) 898-4529
Virginia-Maryland Regional College of Veterinary Medicine, Blacksburg, VA (540) 231-8038
Washington State University, Pullman (509) 335-5704

FINDING HELP ON THE INTERNET

The American Veterinary Medical Association has a listing of grief resources in the Care for Pets section of its Web site: www.avma.org
Animal News: Pet Loss Resource Persons, Counselors, and Groups: www.animalnews.com/memorial/resources.htm
Association for Pet Loss and Bereavement: www.aplb.org
DOGHEAVEN: www.dogheaven.com/about.htm
Forever Pets provides Web-based retail and pet loss resources: www.foreverpets.com
GriefNet: www.griefnet.org
In Memory of Pets tribute page: www.in-memory-of-pets.com/
Pet Chat: www.kathiethaw.com
The Pet Grief Support Website and Candle Ceremony: www.petloss.com
Rainbows Bridge: www.rainbowsbridge.com
Super Dog's Pet Loss Reference Page (for the loss of all animals): www.superdog.com/petloss.htm
The Virtual Pet Cemetery: www.mycemetery.com/my/pet_menu.html

SELECTED BIBLIOGRAPHY

Adamec, Christine. *When Your Pet Dies: Dealing with Your Grief and Helping Your Children Cope.* New York: The Berkley Publishing Group, 1996.

Anderson, Moira. *Coping with Sorrow on the Loss of Your Pet.* 2d ed. Loveland, Colo.: Alpine Publications, 1996.

Antinori, Deborah. *Journey Through Pet Loss.* Basking Ridge, N.J.: Yoko Spirit Publications, 1998, audiocassette.

Bronson, Howard. *Dog Gone: Coping with the Loss of Your Pet.* Mass.: Bestsell Publications, 1994.

Coleman, Joan. *Forever Friends: Resolving Grief after the Loss of a Beloved Animal.* Las Vegas: J.C. Tara Enterprises, 1993.

Colgrove, Melba. et al. *How to Survive the Loss of a Love,* 2nd. ed. Los Angeles: Prelude Press, 1991.

Davis, Christine. *For Every Dog an Angel.* Portland, Oreg.: Lighthearted Press, 1998.

Deits, Bob. *Life After Loss.* 2d ed. Tucson, Ariz.: Fisher Books, 1992.

Gustafson, Mickie. *Losing Your Dog: Coping with Grief when Your Pet Dies.* New York: Bergh Publishing, 1991.

Harris, Eleanor. Pet Loss: *A Spiritual Guide.* St. Paul, Minn.: Llewellyn Publications, 1997.

Hunt, Laurel. *Angel Pawprints. Pasadena, Calif.*: Darrowby Press, 1998.

Ironside, Virginia. *Goodbye, Dear Friend: Coming to Terms with the Death of a Pet.* London: Robson Books, 1994.

James, John and Frank Cherry. *The Grief Recovery Handbook: A Step-by-Step Program for Moving Beyond Loss.* N.Y.: HarperPerennial, 1988.

Johns, Bud ed. *Old Dogs Remembered.* San Francisco: Synergistic Press, 1999.

Johnston, Marianne. *Let's Talk About when Your Pet Dies.* Rosen Publishing Group, 1998.

Kaufman, Julie, D.C. *Crossing the Rubicon: Celebrating the Human-Animal Bond in Life and Death.* Cottage Grove, Wis.: C.A.C. Xenophon Publications, 1999.

Kelleher, Susan. *Spirit Dogs: Heroes in Heaven.* Denver, Colo.: Owl of Athene Press, 1996.

Kosins, Martin. *Maya's First Rose: Diary of a Very Special Love.* Royal Oaks, Mich.: Open Sky Books, 1992.

Kowalski, Gary. *Goodbye, Friend.* Walpole, N.H.: Stillpoint Publishing, International, 1997.

Kurz, Gary. *Cold Noses at the Pearly Gates: A Book of Hope.* Friendswood, Tex., 1997.

Lagoni, Laurel, Carolyn Butler, and Suzanne Hetts, *The Human-Animal Bond and Grief.* Philadelphia: W.B. Saunders, 1994.

Lemieux, Christina M. *Coping with the Loss of a Pet: A Gentle Guide for All Who Love a Pet.* Reading, Pa.: Wallace R. Clark Publishers, 1988.

Maria L. Quintana. et al. *It's Okay to Cry.* rev. ed. Perrysburg, Ohio: Mariposa Press, 1998.

Milani, Myrna M. *Preparing for the Loss of Your Pet: Saying Goodbye with Love, Dignity, and Peace of Mind.* Rocklin, Calif.: Prima Publishing, 1998.

Montgomery, Mary, and Herb, Montgomery. *Goodbye My Friend.* Minneapolis: Montgomery Press, 1991.

Nieberg, Herbert, Ph.D. *Pet Loss: A Thoughtful Guide for Adults and Children.* New York: Harper & Row, 1996.

Peterson, Linda, ed. *Surviving the Heartbreak of Choosing Death for Your Pet.* West Chester, Pa.: Greentree Publishing, 1997.

Potter, J., Jr., and George Koss. *Death of a Pet: Answers to Questions for Children and Animal Lovers of All Ages.* Stamford, N.Y.: Guideline Publications, 1991.

Quackenbush, Jamie, and Denise Graveline. *When Your Pet Dies: How to Cope with Your Feelings.* New York: Simon & Schuster, 1985.

Ross, Cheri Barton. et al. *Pet Loss and Human Emotion: Guiding Clients Through Grief.* Accelerated Development, 1998.

Shaw, Eva. *What To Do When a Loved One Dies.* Irvine, Calif.: Dickens Press, 1994.

Sife, Wallace, Ph.D. *The Loss of a Pet.* rev. ed. N.Y.: Howell Book House, 1998.

Stern, Michael, and Susan Cropper. *Loving and Losing a Pet: A Psychologist and a Veterinarian Share Their Wisdom.* Northvale, N.J.: Jason Aronson, Inc., 1998.

Stuparyk, Emily Margaret. *When Only the Love Remains: The Pain of Pet Loss.* Canada: Hushion House, 1999.

Tousley, Marty, and Katherine Heuerman. *The Final Farewell.* Phoenix, Ariz.: Our Pals Publishing Co., 1997.

Townsend, Irving. *Separate Lifetimes.* Townsend Publications, 1986.

Traisman, Enid. *My Personal Pet Remembrance Journal.* Direct Book Service, 1995.

Wagner, Teresa L., and Maxine Musgrave. *Legacies of Love: A Gentle Guide to Healing from the Loss of Your Animal Loved One.* 1998, audiocassette.

Walker, Kaetheryn. *The Heart That Is Loved Never Forgets.* Rochester, Vt.: Healing Arts Press, 1999.

Watson, George, and Emily Watson. *Dogs Have Souls Too: The Spirit of Miss Sarah.* Salt Lake City, Utah: PMD Publishing, 2000.

BOOKS FOR OR ABOUT CHILDREN

Brown, Margaret. *The Dead Bird.* New York: HarperCollins, 1983.

Buscaglia, Leo. *The Fall of Freddie the Leaf: A Story of Life for All Ages.* New York: Holt, Rinehart & Winston, 1982.

Greenberg, Judith E., and Helen H.Carey. *Sunny: The Death of a Pet.* New York: Franklin Watts, 1986.

Grollman, Earl. *Bereaved Children and Teens: A Support Guide for Parents and Professionals.* Beacon Press, 1995.

Grollman, Earl. *Talking About Death: A Dialog Between Parent and Child.* Beacon Press, 1990.

Mellonie, Brian, and Robert Ingpen. *Lifetimes: The Beautiful Way to Explain Death to Children.* New York: Bantam Books, 1983.

Moorhead, Debby. *A Special Place for Charles: A Child's Companion Through Pet Loss.* Broomfield, Colo.: Partners in Publishing, 1996.

Napoli, Donna Jo. *The Bravest Thing.* New York: Dutton Children's Books, 1995.

Rogers, Fred. *When a Pet Dies.* New York: Putnam Publishing group, 1988.

Simon, Norma. *The Saddest Time.* Albert Whitman Press, 1986.

Stolz, Mary. *King Emmett the Second.* New York: Greenwillow Books, 1991.

Tester, Sylvia Root. *Sad (What Does It Mean?).* Elgin Ill.: The Child's World, 1980.

Thomas, Jane Resh. *The Comeback Dog.* New York: Bantam-Skylark, 1984.

Tousley, Marty. *Children and Pet Loss: A Guide for Helping.* Scottsdale, Ariz.: Companion Animal Association of Arizona, 1996.

VanderWyden, William. *Butterflies: Talking with Children about Death and Life Eternal.* Tabor Publishing, 1991.

Warburg, Sandol. *Growing Time.* New York: Houghton-Mifflin, 1989.

Wilhelm, Hans. *I'll Always Love You.* New York: Crown Publishers, 1985.

MISCELLANEOUS RESOURCES

Avanti Press sells pet loss sympathy cards: (313) 961-0022

E-mail sympathy cards can be found at Pet Loss: Tracks in the Sand: www.members.tripod.com/~Sandtracker/cat-tracks.html

TreeGivers Pet Memorial Tree Planting (800) 862-TREE; www.treegivers.com/program.html

World Animal Net is the largest network of animal protection societies with over 1,500 affiliates in more than 80 countries campaigning to improve the status and welfare of animals: www.worldanimal.net

Choosing a pet cemetery as the final resting place for your loyal friend may help you find comfort in knowing your pets' remains are in a safe and secure environment. The yellow pages are a good place to start looking for a pet cemetery in your area. Veterinary clinics may also share such information with you. You may contact the International Association of Pet Cemeteries (IAPC) at PO Box 163, Ellenburg Depot, New York 12935, (518) 594-3000 for information on pet cemeteries in your area.

Founded in 1971 by Pat Blosser, the IAPC is a not-for-profit organization dedicated to the advancement of pet cemeteries through public awareness programs. The IAPC is comprised of dedicated people who work for the good of the industry and the public. It operates on a budget that is supported by dues and other contributions from members—there are no paid directors—and all efforts are voluntary. Member pet cemeteries are expected to maintain the highest business and ethical standards. Through education and cooperation with pet cemeteries, crematories, funeral homes, veterinary services, and pet-related societies, associations, manufacturers, and suppliers, the organization serves the needs of the general public and the entire pet aftercare industry.

Every effort has been made to provide accurate information on the following list of pet cemeteries. Most of the locations are members of the IAPC. Before making your pet's final arrangements, please remember to contact and visit the cemetery you have in mind to be sure it's the best resting place for your animal companion.

ALABAMA

Alabama Pet Cemetery
Highway 78
Brompton, AL 35209
205-870-5010

ALASKA

Harthaven Pet Cremation Services
2518 East Tudor Road, Suite #203
Anchorage, AK 99507
907-563-1801

ARIZONA

PALS—Pet & Animal Lovers Service
3629 North 40th Avenue
Phoenix, AZ 85019
602-455-6677
www.ourpals.com

The Pet Cemetery of Tucson
5720 East Glenn Street
Tucson, AZ 85712
520-566-4242

Sunland Pet Rest
10917 Sunland Drive
Sun City, AZ 85351
623-933-0560

CALIFORNIA

AA Sorrento Valley Pet Cemetery and Crematory
10801 Sorrento Valley Road
San Diego, CA 92121
760-276-3361

Bubbling Well Pet Memorial Park
2462 Atlas Peak Road
Napa, CA 94558
707-255-3456
www.bubbling-well.com

Franklin Pet Cemetery and Valley Crematory
2405 Ashby Road
Merced, CA 95348
209-383-4582

Monterey Bay Memorial Park
885 Strawberry Road
Royal Oaks, CA 95076
831-722-8722

Pet's Rest Cemetery, Crematory for Pet Animals
1905 Hillside Boulevard
Colma, CA 94014
650-755-2201
www.petsrest.com

San Diego Pet Memorial Park
8995 Crestmar Point
San Diego, CA 92121
858-271-4242
www.sandiegopetmemorial.com

Sea Breeze Pet Cemetery
19542 Beach Boulevard
Huntington Beach, CA 92648
714-962-7111

Sierra Hills Pet Cemetery
6700 Verner Avenue
Sacramento, CA 95841
916-732-2037

CANADA

Cherished Pets Memorial Services
4 Neck Road
Summerville,NB, CAN E5S 1V8
506-763-2252

Country Club Pet Resort and Memorial Park
Range Road 282
Calgary, Alberta, CAN T2P 2G6
403-936-5685

Devonshire Pet Memorial Services
146 Major's Path
St. Johns, NF, CAN A1A 5A1
709-754-2340

Domestic Animal Cremation
Highway 26
St. Francois Xavier, Mb., CAN R4L 1A2
204-864-2815

Gateway Pet Memorial Services
180 Southgate Drive, Unit 3
Guelph, Ont., CAN N1G 4P5
519-822-8858

Misty Gardens Pet Cemetery
Floodway Drive
La Salle, Mb., CAN
204-736-4727

Sandy Ridge Pet Cemetery
11210 Ridge Line
Eden, Ont., CAN NOJ 1HO
519-866-3243
www.sandyrpetcem.com

Veterinary Referral Cremation Service
905 Pembroke Street East
Pembroke, Ont., CAN K8A 3M3
613-732-3641

COLORADO

Denver Pet Cemetery and Crematory
5721 East 72nd Avenue
Commerce City, CO 80022
303-288-0177

Evergreen Pet Cemetery at
Evergreen Memorial Park
26624 North Turkey Creek Road
Evergreen, CO 80439
303-674-7777

Final Paws Pet Cemetery
and Crematory
356B Ridge Circle Drive
Grand Junction, CO 81503
970-242-7417

CONNECTICUT

Balmoral Pet Cemetery
774 Kent Road
Gaylordsville, CT 06755
860-354-3433

Forest Rest Memorial Park
2811 Hebron Avenue
Glastonbury, CT 06033
860-659-0784

Keystone Memorial Park
Pet Cemetery
227 Cheshire Road
Bethany, CT 06524
203-393-3126

Trail's End Pet Cemetery
and Crematory
706 Horsehill Road
Westbrook, CT 06498
860-399-5420

ENGLAND

The Surrey Pet Cemetery
and Crematorium
Byers Lane, South Godstone
Surrey, ENG RH9 8JL
(01342) 893069

FLORIDA

Broward Pet Cemetery
and Crematory
11455 North West Eighth Street
Plantation, FL 33325
954-476-0743

Driftwood Pet Memorial Gardens
800 East Laurel Road
Laurel, FL 34272
941-485-6672

Hartsdale Pet Cemetery
and Crematory
Hartsdale, New York

E. W. Russo—Pet Cremation Network
8084 North Davis Highway, PMB 140
Pensacola, FL 32514
850-477-2563
www.petcremation.cc

Garden of Love Pet Memorial Park
Highway 441 South
Micanopy, FL 32667
352-377-7455

Greenbrier Memory Gardens for Pets
3703 West Kelly Park Road
Apopka, FL 32712
407-886-2620

Jancy Pet Burial Service
4596 Laughlin Road
Zellwood, FL 32798
407-884-7336

Noah's Ark Boarding Kennel
and Pet Cemetery
3725 Marsh Road
DeLand, FL 32724
904-736-9848

Oak Lawn Pet Cemetery at
The Humane Society of Greater Miami
2101 North West 95th Street
Miami, FL 33147
305-696-0800
www.humanesocietymiami.org

Pet Heaven Memorial Park
10901 West Flagler Street
Miami, FL 33174
305-223-6515

Pinellas Memorial Pet Cemetery
and Crematory
6500 86th Avenue North
Pinellas Park, FL 33782
727-544-1051

Twin Oaks Pet Cemetery
and Crematorium
251 North East 300th Street
Okeechobee, FL 34972
863-467-6377
www.twin-oak.com

GEORGIA

Atlanta Pet Cemetery and Crematory
4964-A Atlanta Road
Atlanta, GA 30080
770-333-3332
www.apetcc.com

Deceased Pet Care Funeral Home
and Crematory
4991 Peachtree Road
Chamblee, GA 30341
770-457-7659

Loving Care Pet Cemetery
3470 Pope Road
Douglasville, GA 30135
770-457-7659

Memory Gardens for Pets
Funeral Home, Crematory
and Cemetery
2751 Highway 441
Watkinsville, GA 30677
706-769-7386 or 800-925-6117

Oak Rest Pet Gardens
Funeral Home and Crematory
2691 Harbins Road
Bethlehem, GA 30620
770-995-8862

Savannah Pet Cemetery
9 Salt Creek Road
Savannah, GA 31405
912-233-3767

IOWA

Loving Rest Pet Funeral Home
Cemetery/Crematory
992 G24 Highway
Indianola, IA 50125
515-962-1099

Pet Memories Funeral Home
and Crematory Services
618 235th Street
Tipton, IA 52772
877-822-7387

ILLINOIS

Aarrowood Pet Cemetery and Crematory
24090 North Highway 45
Vernon Hills, IL 60061
847-634-3787

Fawnwoods of Windridge Memorial Park
7014 South Rawson Bridge Road
Cary, IL 60013
847-639-3883

Garden of Faithful Friends within
Sunset Hill Memorial Estates Cemetery
2900 South State Route 157
Edwardsville, IL 62025
618-656-3220
www.sunsethillcemetery.com

Hinsdale Animal Cemetery
6400 South Bentley Avenue
Willowbrook, IL 60514
630-323-5120
www.petcemetery.org

Kirlin-Egan and Butler Funeral Home
and Cremation Tribute
907 South 7th Street
Springfield, IL 62703
217-544-4646
www.kirlin-egan-butler.com

Paw Print Gardens Pet Cemetery
and Crematory
27 West 150 North Avenue
West Chicago, IL 60185
630-231-1117
www.pawprintpetcemetery.com

INDIANA

The Farm Pet Cemetery
2375 North New Salem Road
Salem, IN 47167
812-967-3547

Memory Gardens Cemetery for Pets
9055 Pendleton Pike
Indianapolis, IN 46236
317-895-9055

Peaceful Pets Cemetery
1325 Mackey Ferry Road
Mount Vernon, IN 47620
812-838-0811
www.peacefulpets.com

MAINE

Blueberry Ridge Pet Crematory
1117 Maine Road
Eddington, ME 04428
207-843-5331

MARYLAND

Dulaney Pet Haven
200 East Padonia Road
Timonium, MD 21093
410-666-0495

Resthaven Memorial Gardens
7401 US Route 15 North
Fredrick, MD 21701
301-898-7177

Sugarloaf Pet Gardens
21511 Peach Tree Road, Box 415
Barnesville, MD 20838
301-972-8555
www.sugarloafpetgardens.com

Valley Pet Cemetery
and Crematory
127 Britner Avenue
Williamsport, MD 21795
301-582-3320

MASSACHUSETTS

Angel View Pet Cemetery
465 Wareham Street, Route 28
Middleboro, MA 02346
508-947-4103
www.angelview.com

MICHIGAN

AAA Dog and Cat Cemetery
25280 Pennsylvania Road
Taylor, MI 48180
734-946-5555
www.aaapet.com

Country Meadows Pet Cemetery
5401 North Michigan Road, M-99
Dimondale, MI 48821
517-646-8043

Harperlawn Pet Memorial Gardens
33711 Harper Avenue
Clinton Township, Michigan 48035
810-792-3030

Noah's Gardens Pet
Cemetery-Mortuary
2727 Orange Avenue, South East
Grand Rapids, MI 49546
616-949-1390

Precious Pets Pet Crematory, Burial
Services and Memorial Merchandise
2012 Portage Road
Kalamazoo, MI 49001
616-388-7387
www.preciouspet.com

MISSISSIPPI

Pet Paradise
369 Johns Hopkins Drive
Jackson, MS
601-922-9222

MISSOURI

Order of the Golden Rule
13523 Lakefront Drive
Bridgeton, MO 63045
314-209-7142

NEBRASKA

Rolling Acres Pet Cemetery,
Crematory and Funeral Home
400 South 134th Street
Lincoln, NE 68520
402-483-7001

NEW JERSEY

Pet Lawn Memorial Park
591 Route 73 North
West Berlin, NJ 08091
856-767-1564
www.abn1.net/petlawn

NEW MEXICO

Best Friends Pet Cremation Services
3816 Edith North East
Albuquerque, NM 87107
505-345-5615

NEVADA

Craig Road Pet Cemetery,
Funeral Home and Crematoriums
7450 West Craig Road
Las Vegas, NV 89129
702-645-1112
www.craigroadpetcemetery.com

Sierra Vista Pet Cemetery
and Crematorium
3770 Butti Way
Carson City, NV 89701
775-887-2171

NEW YORK

Abbingdon Hill Pet Animal
Cemetery and Crematory
148 Youngblood Road
Montgomery, NY 12549
914-361-2200

Drownwood Forest Pet Cemetery,
Crematory and Mausoleum
5055 Route 11
West Chazy, NY 12992
518-594-7500

Faithful Companion Pet Memorial Park
568 Violet Avenue
Hyde Park, NY 12538
914-452-1654

Hartsdale Pet Cemetery and Crematory
75 North Central Park Avenue
Hartsdale, NY 10530
914-949-2583

My Pet Memorial Park Subsidiary of
Stevens Swan Humane Society
10100 Church Road
Utica, NY 13502
315-732-8440

Pet Crematory Agency
164 Cabot Street
West Babylon, NY 11704
631-293-2929
www.petcrematory.com

Pet Haven Cemetery
and Crematory
4501-3 West Seneca Turnpike
Syracuse, NY 13215
315-469-1212

Regency Forest Pet Memorial
Funeral Home, Cemetery
and Crematory
760 Middle Country Road
Middle Island, NY 11953
631-345-0600 or 800-372-PETS

Rolling Acres Pet Cemetery
1365 Tamarac Road
Troy, NY 12181
518-663-5122

Rush Inter Pet Cemetery
and Crematory
139 Rush Road
West Rush, NY 14543
716-533-1685

Saratoga Pet Cemetery
796 Route 9
Wilton, NY 12831
518-587-2662

Whispering Pines
Pet Cemetery
Gardner Road
Binghamton, NY 13903
607-565-7297

NORTH CAROLINA

Good Shepherd Pet Crematory
and Cemetery
5198 NC Highway 211
West End, NC 27376
910-673-2200

Lynaire Crematory
4634 Old Cherry Point Road
New Bern, NC 28560
252-633-6225

Saint Francis Pet Funeral Service
and Cemetery
3903 Hunt Chase Drive
Jamestown, NC 27282
336-886-7387

OHIO

Angel Refuge Pet Cemetery
and Crematory
2726 Park Avenue West
Ontario, OH 44906
419-529-2229

Bayliff and Son Pet Crematory
311 West Main Street
Cridersville, OH 45806
419-645-6700

Karnik Memorial Gardens
5411 Black Road
Waterville, OH 43566
419-878-9796

Paws Awhile Pet
Memorial Park, Crematory
and Funeral Home
3426 Brush Road
Richfield, OH 44286
330-659-4270

Pet Cremation Services
888 Frank Road West
Columbus, OH 43223
614-272-6550

Rome Pet Cemetery
21993 State Route 243
Proctorville, OH 45669
740-886-9888

Western Farm Pet Crematory
and Cemetery
12521 South Island Road
Grafton, OH 44044
440-748-1716

Woodside Pet Cemetery
6450 Shepler Church Road, South West
Navarre, OH 44662
330-484-1997

OKLAHOMA

Precious Pets Cemetery
and Crematory
5510 North Spencer Road
Spencer, OK 73084
405-771-5510
www.preciouspetscemetery.com

OREGON

Green Acres Pet Cemetery
and Crematorium
1849 North Phoenix Road
Medford, OR 97504
541-773-6199

PENNSYLVANIA

Buck's County Pet Cemetery
1765 Old Bethlehem Road
Quakertown, PA 18951
215-257-9584

Chestnut Ridge Pet Cemetery
609 East Market Street
Blairsville, PA 15717
724-459-7750

Faithful Companions Pet Cemetery
and Crematory
RD#2, Box 210, Burlington Road
East Smithfield, PA 18817
570-596-3192

Faithful Pets Memorial Gardens
693 New Salem Road
Uniontown, PA 15401
724-245-8524

Forever Friends Pet Memorial Park
12670 Foust Road
Conneaut Lake, PA 16316
814-382-5446

Hearthside Rest Pet Cemetery
3024 West 26th Street
Erie, PA 16506
814-838-7638

Lacey Memorial Pet Cemetery
R 1000 South Church Street
Hazleton, PA 18201
570-454-6655

Pennsylvania SPCA
Box 226, Route 6
Wellsboro, PA 16901
570-724-3687

Pet Memorial Funeral Home
and Crematory
128 Hazelwood Avenue
Pittsburgh, PA 15207
412-421-6910

Pet Rest Memorial Park
RR3, 8th St.
Watsonville, PA 17777
570-538-2008

SOUTH CAROLINA

Midlands Pet Care
4948 Highway 378
Lexington, SC 29071
803-356-1610

Pet Rest Cemetery and Cremation Service
Old Highway 52 (Cypress Gardens Rd.)
Goose Creek, SC 29445
843-797-5735
www.petrestcarolina.com

TENNESSEE

Dixie Memorial
Pet Cemetery
7960 Epperson Mill Road
Millington, TN 38053
901-873-4127

Cedar Hills Pet Cemetery
2467 Nashville Highway
Columbia, TN 38401
931-486-3255

Pet Haven Cemetery and Crematory
10088 Standifer Gap Road
Ooltewah, TN 37363
423-396-9877

TEXAS

Bit of Heaven Pet Cemetery
and Crematorium
8726 Congo Lane
Houston, TX 77040
713-690-7449

Faithful Friends Pet Cemetery
and Crematory
3600 Shelby Road
Fort Worth, TX 76140
817-478-6696

God's Creatures
Pet Crematory
11307 China Spring Road
Waco, TX 76708
254-836-4484

Paws In Heaven
Pet Crematory
2106 Sattler Road
Canyon Lake, TX 78132
830-964-2210

Rolling Hills Pet Cemetery
and Crematory
503 North Ann Boulevard
Harkers Heights, TX 76543
254-699-6365

Toothacres Pet Cemetery and Crematory
1632 Parker Road
North Carrolton, TX 75008
972-492-3711

VIRGINIA

Faithful Friends Pet Cemetery
6217 Memorial Drive
Sandston, VA 23150
804-737-6006

WASHINGTON

ARK Northwest Pet Memorial
and Crematorium
14606 Pacific Avenue South, Suite D
Tacoma, WA 98444
253-536-8775

WISCONSIN

Forrest Run Pet Cemetery
and Crematory
West 5123 Natures Way Drive
Sherwood, WI 54169
920-989-2600

Lakeview Memorial Park
2786 Algoma Boulevard
Oshkosh, WI 54901
920-236-2828

Peaceful Hills Pet Cemetery
5059 County Road K
Hartford, WI 53027
262-644-8996

Peaceful Pines Pet Memorial Park
168 Lois Lane
Mosinee, WI 54455
715-693-4693

Petland Memorial Garden
2786 Algoma Boulevard
Oshkosh, WI 54901
920-236-2828

WYOMING

Angel Companions Pet Cemetery
and Crematorium
3639 Cattle Trail Drive
Casper, WY 82604
307-237-5744
www.angelcompanions.com

San Diego Pet Memorial Park
San Diego, California

The photographs in this book were

taken with a 35mm camera, using color slide film—Fuji Velvia, Kodachrome, and Kodak Color Infrared. There are a few images in which I rephotographed an already printed photo, which can be found on pages 4, 6, and 16, that came from my family archives. The large bleed images are direct reproductions of my original slides. The small format images are direct reproductions of the photographs I printed through the Polaroid Image Transfer process.

My idea for this book was to present you with a precious little piece that would closely depict the precious little graves and animal images I saw in my travels. I felt that the Polaroid Image Transfer process was the most appropriate way to deliver my personal experience and feelings to you.

There is no specific set of instructions to follow when making image transfers. Experimentation, trial and error, and patience are key. The book *Polaroid Transfers* written by Kathleen Thormod Carr was a valuable resource, and the Polaroid Corporation's generous gift of film helped tremendously. To create these images, I placed my original slide into an enlarger or a Daylab Jr. machine. Then I projected the image onto Polaroid 669 film, pulled the film through it's holder, and before the image fully developed onto it's paper, I peeled the negative and positive apart and rolled the negative face down onto another piece of paper such as hot, wet, vinegared, watercolor paper. The end result is a photograph that has fully developed on a different recepter surface. When finally peeling the negative away from the watercolor paper, the inconsistent edges and emulsion liftoff add to the surrrealistic beauty of these miniature photographic paintings. In many cases, I enhanced the surreal effect by adding watercolor washes, ink, or pastels. I hope you enjoy looking at them as much as I enjoyed creating them.

Billy Altomare
At age 3